Contents

01

CHAPTER

01

Authority

Just because you have the
authority to do something,
doesn't mean you have to use it.

Be patient and humble, and when the time is
right, you'll know when to execute it,

Being the person in charge comes with more
than a title or paycheck. You have to do the
work. You have to know the job of every person
that reports to you.

Authority

People don't do what you expect them to do, people do what you inspect them to do.

Treat everyone the same. The only difference between you and the people that reports to you are the titles.

Everyone deserves to be treated with respect no matter where they are in life. Never look down on someone unless you are reaching down to help them up

CHAPTER

Becoming an Effective Leader

You can't expect great results with only half the effort. Write the plan. Check the plan. Check the plan again. Put your plan into action. Manifest the plan.

In order to be an exceptional Leader, you must be an exceptional follower. There is something for us to learn each and every day. Never get so high up, that you stop learning, and you stop listening. An exceptional Leader, leads by demonstrating, not by delegating.

Becoming an Effective Leader

Before you get angry with someone in any situation, think of how that person may have perceived you in that scenario. Don't let anger control you. You can accomplish more with a humble spirit or demeanor than you can with an angry approach.

If someone offends you, let it go. You can't get them like God can. Let God be your Guide and your Strategy. Follow His instructions. Trust His Process. God will never allow you to be side swiped by anything or anyone.

CHAPTER

The Company You Keep

Watch the company you keep. Those closest to you, are the ones who can and or will attempt to destroy everything about you. Only keep people around that support you in the same manner that you support them. These people are rare, and cannot be replaced.

In order for you to become all that God has called you to be, you will need to take inventory of those around you. It may be hard, but you will need to seperate yourself from the people, places, and things, that goes against God's Purpose for your life.

The Company You Keep

Only allow those that are not afraid to see you succeed into your circle. The ones that inspire you, help nurture your Calling/Purpose, encourage your growth, and want to see you win. The ones that, when you get knocked down, don't allow you to stay down.

Be aware of the people who only want you to win at the level they feel you should be successful at. Stick to the plan that God has placed on your heart. He gave you the vision and no one else.

CHAPTER

Accountability

The one person you have to show up for each day is yourself. Holding yourself accountable for your own actions is the first step to becoming a great leader. When we are not afraid to admit our faults, we allow ourselves the necessary room we'll need to grow in order to advance.

Holding ourselves accountable first, will set the tone for the environment and atmosphere we wish to create for those we are given the opportunity to lead.

Accountability

Accountability is something we must work on each and every day. When we take ownership for our own actions, we are teaching others in our paths, the difference between right and wrong.

Each day we wake up, we should be a better person than we were the day before. It is a continuing process to look at ourselves in the mirror and know that we are not perfect, but striving everyday.

CHAPTER

Listening

Listening is one of the most important aspects of Leadership. Listening requires one's undivided attention and affective interpretation.

When we engage in conversation with one another, we must listen to understand instead of listening to make a response.

Listening

When we listen to respond, not only have we dismissed key details of the conversation, we've missed the opportunity to connect with the individual and the core reason for them expressing themselves.

When we listen to understand, we give heed to verbal and nonverbal feedback. We take notice of the attributes instead of our preconceived notions of the situation.

CHAPTER

Integrity

Live the life you display in front of people, behind closed doors

There is nothing worse than being a walking contradiction.

Always choose to do right, never uphold wrong. You don't ever want to be in a place where compromising with wrong becomes a normal substitute for right.

Leaders raise other Leaders. What type of Leadership will you teach? Which kind of Leaders will you train up?

Integrity

True Leaders, lead by example. Never think that you're so high, that you forget what it felt like when you were being taught or when you had your own struggles.

Remain coachable and teachable. There's nothing worse than always being the smartest person in the room. When we get to the point where no one can tell or teach us anything, it becomes exasperating.

07

CHAPTER

07

Consistency

"You Gotta Want It". Feed your dreams and goals. Starve your distractions. Work on you everyday. Set attainable goals for yourself to accomplish within a certain timeframe.

Be persistent with what you want. Always envision yourself in the place you desire to be. Keep your mind on the end result while living in the present.

Consistency

Set aside some quiet time so that you are able to work on your goals without distractions. This time can be spent in meditation, reading, journaling, or whatever you need to do to accomplish your goals.

Fight the urge to want to fall back into old routines and habits. Work on one project at a time, so that you do not become overwhelmed.
Remain: True
Humble
Grateful

CHAPTER

Lessons Learned

Meditate Daily

Be an Original

Petty is not the answer

When we learn better, let's do better

Never take on too many tasks at once

Learn how to say "No"

Keep an open mind

Do your research, don't take others word as solid facts

Lessons Learned

Read Everyday

Never stop Learning

Make it Make Sense

Show Compassion

Allow Love to be Your Core

Be willing to deal with the consequences of your actions

You have to want it

Change Your Mindset, Change Your Lifestyle

Notes

Notes

Notes

www.ingramcontent.com/pod-product-compliance
Lightning Source LLC
LaVergne TN
LVHW010026070426
835509LV00001B/27